GENERAL INFORMATION

WHAT ARE HERMIT CRABS?

Phylum Arthropoda: Animals with specialized body segments, hardened exoskeletons, and jointed appendages

Subphylum Diantennata: Arthropods with a pair of mandibles that flank the mouth and at least one pair of antennae.

Class Crustacea: Diantennata with two pairs of antennae and double-branched (biramous) appendages.

Order Decapoda: Crustacea with five pairs of legs.

Infraorder Anomura: Decapoda, with reduced fifth pair of thoracic legs and the folded up bases above the bases of the fourth pair of legs.

Family Coenobitidae: Land hermit crabs.

TAXONOMY

Land Hermit crabs are crustaceans in the family Coenobitidae which includes all the land hermit crabs. The family consists of two genera, *Coenobita* with eleven species including the common land hermit crab of the pet trade, and the monotypic robber or coconut crab *Birgus latro,* the largest land dwelling crab/arthropod.

The land hermit crab commonly sold in the pet trade is the West Atlantic land hermit crab and has the scientific name of *Coenobita clypeatus.*

Besides land hermit crabs, there are species of intertidal hermit crabs in the family Diogenidae and several families of sea-dwelling hermit crabs.

A large specimen of land hermit crab carrying a turbo snail shell. As the hermit the crabs get larger it becomes increasingly difficult for them to find large shells in the wild.

After this land hermit crab died, the shell was clipped off with cutting pliers to expose how a hermit crab positions itself in a shell. This specimen was so large that it could not withdraw it's legs or head in the shell. The abdomen barely fit in the shell and little water could be stored. A good shell that holds water will make a land hermit crab seem heavy when picked up.

ANATOMY
Crustaceans have a very different anatomy than mammalian vertebrates and a special terminology is used to describe their anatomical parts. Hermit crabs have two main body segments: the cephalothorax, which is a fusion of the head and thorax (midsection), and the soft abdomen. In the land hermit crab, the soft abdomen twists to the right side to allow it to lodge itself within the shell of a gastropod (sea snail).

In the very front of the crab's body you will notice two eyes connected to the body by eye stalks. Just below the eyes are two pairs of antennae — a pair of regular antennae and a pair of antennules with bent tips. Beneath the two pairs of antennae are the mouth parts. Noteworthy are the elongated leg-like mouth parts called the *third maxillipeds*, used during eating and grooming of antennae.

A hermit crab has five pairs of legs, a pair of large claws which in biology are called *chelipeds* or *chelae* (the singular is *chela*) and four pairs of *walking legs*. The left claw is larger than the right claw and is used for defense and during locomotion. The smaller right claw is used during eating and drinking to transfer material to the mouth. The front two pairs of walking legs are kept outside the shell and used for walking. The back two pairs of walking legs are kept in the shell and used to anchor the crab inside its shell, perform grooming activities, and function in the course of reproduction.

DISTRIBUTION
The West Atlantic land hermit crab that is commonly sold in the pet trade has a wide range in nature, from southern Florida and the Bahamas through the West Indies to Venezuela.

SIZE

West Atlantic hermit crabs grow to about four ounces (110 grams) body weight. Very old large specimens can weigh more than seven ounces (200 grams) and measure more than six inches (15 cm) long.

Note: From this point on West Atlantic land hermit crabs, which are the primary topic of this book, will be referred to as simply land hermit crabs or hermit crabs.

HOW LONG DO LAND HERMIT CRABS LIVE?

Most land hermit crabs die while in the aquatic larval stage. Only a small percentage of those who make it to land become breeding adults. It takes about two years for a land hermit crab to become a sexually mature adult. For a long, healthy life, a critical limiting factor is the availability of large suitable shells. Few large shells are available, and there is strong competition between large hermit crabs for these shells. Nonetheless, if food and large shells are available, a land hermit crab can continue to grow for many years, with giant specimens weighing up to seven ounces (200 grams) and estimated to be at least 30 years old.

In captivity, most hermit crabs are dead within a year mostly because they are not kept under the right conditions. However a small percentage will live for several years with reports of some specimens living ten or more years in captivity.

HABITS

The general pattern of larger hermit crabs is to rest in shelters, under litter, or partially burrowed during the day and to become active at night when the temperature is cooler and there are fewer predators. Smaller

Top view showing cephalothorax, abdomen curled to the right, claws, legs, antennae, and antennules. The anus is located at the end of the abdomen.

hermit crabs are commonly found close to shore where small shells are abundant. They may be active during the day.

Gill

In this undissected hermit crab, the posterior opening of the branchial (gill) chamber is shown by the inserted forceps. Shell water is obtained through dipping and water expelled through the branchial chamber. Notice how some of the posterior gills are exposed.

Branchial chamber

Gills

Here a lateral section of the cephalothoracic exoskeleton has been removed to expose the branchial chamber and the gills.

SELECTION OF LAND HERMIT CRABS

Hermit crabs are now sold in many pet stores, gift shops and stands along coastal boardwalks. Because hermit crabs are often scaled in their shells during the day, your opportunity for selection will usually be limited. Good general rules are:

1) Avoid limp sluggish hermit crabs that are partially or completely out of their shells and hang loosely when you pick them up. Healthy hermit crabs either withdraw into their shells or are out and active with antennae fluttering and claws ready to pinch. Sick hermit crabs can initially still be withdrawn in the shell but upon emergence are sluggish and demonstrate little fluttering of antennae.

2) Select hermit crabs that feel heavy when picked up. Light hermit crabs may be dehydrated or sick.

3) If there are many dead hermit crabs or crabs partially out of their shells, avoid buying a crab from that enclosure. It could be sick or seriously dehydrated.

4) Some hermit crabs are missing limbs or the ends of limbs. Most of these will survive and regenerate their missing limbs after a few molts but, given the opportunity, you might as well select animals with perfect appearances.

5) Pick animals that are active and vigorous, with fluttering antennae and quick withdrawal responses. Animals that are feeding well are generally good choices.

6) Inspect the crabs for mites that appear as tiny light-colored arthropods seen crawling about the crab. Avoid mite-infested crabs.

7) Size is a significant factor in selection. If you can only afford a small enclosure, stick to small crabs. The large ones need at least a 20-gallon tank. Large crabs are also messier and more destructive, so if you are interested in a nice display, smaller crabs are a better choice. Size is also a consideration if you want to handle your hermit crabs. For this purpose start off with small hermit crabs. They won't pinch as hard and won't be able to pinch as much skin. If you want larger hermit crabs, purchase sizeable ones to start with because hermit crabs simply do not grow that quickly.

HOW MANY HERMIT CRABS?
It is a good idea when possible to get more than one hermit crab. Aim for six small hermit crabs (1-1½ inches) per ten gallon setup, possibly more if you are buying very small specimens. You can keep up to four large land hermit crabs in a 20 gallon tank.

If kept singly, a hermit crab will easily be lost in a large enclosure and will not be especially entertaining. You will be dependent on its level of activity for all opportunities of observation. If you have several hermit crabs, however, you'll be able to observe more hermit crabs involved in various activities. Some will climb and rest on wood, others may remain at ground level, and still others may burrow. In the evening, hermit crabs may gather in groups in a feeding dish and communicate by tapping their shells or stridulating (making noise by rubbing legs together). Simply said, a small group of hermit crabs are a lot more fun to own than just one.

CANNIBALISM
Cannibalism has been reported in land hermit crabs. Large specimens may eat smaller ones. Hermits that have just molted are particularly vulnerable because of their soft exoskeleton, as are shell-less crabs that have been unable to find a suitable shell. To prevent cannibalism, you need only to:
- keep crabs together that are in the same size range;
- provide a burrowing medium for molting;
- make available a good selection of extra shells; and
- keep your hermit crabs well fed.

PERSONALITIES
Surprisingly enough, even creatures as primitive as hermit crabs will display variations in personality. Some will withdraw into their shell at the drop of a hat. Others will more readily emerge from their shell when picked up. Some pinch readily. Others are more reluctant to pinch their handlers. Some are more lively and outgoing, while others are very secretive.

A basic setup with sand, two water dishes, and wood for shelters and climbing.

SELECTION AND DESIGN OF ENCLOSURES

There are two ways to keep hermit crabs:

THE WRONG WAY

For short life spans, hermit crabs are kept by what I call the prison approach. In a nutshell, this is keeping a hermit crab in a small plastic terrarium where it can barely move and where it will usually die after a few months. These crabs die because their small containers make it impossible to provide what they need. Besides being a death sentence, the prison approach makes it impossible for a hermit crab to behave normally because the container is too small. There is no room to climb or to burrow, and barely enough room for food and water. Obviously, I don't recommend this method for keeping hermit crabs.

...AND THE RIGHT WAY

The other method makes the assumption that no one knows better what a hermit crab needs than a hermit crab. It provides a variety of conditions from which a hermit crab is allowed to select what it wants. Because providing a variety of conditions, much as one finds in nature, requires space, at least a ten-gallon and preferably a 20-gallon all-glass aquarium will be required to keep small specimens. For larger hermit crabs, at least a 20-gallon tank and preferably a more spacious one will be required. If you must have a plastic terrarium, then buy the largest one you can afford. Recently, wire cages have been offered for keeping hermit crabs. These are unsuitable except in warm, humid areas of the U.S. such as Florida, and in warm, humid countries. If you decide to use wire caging you will have to include a container for a burrowing/molting medium (see Burrowing/Molting substrate below).

WHERE TO KEEP YOUR HERMIT CRAB ENCLOSURE

Hermit crabs are best kept out of bedrooms unless you are a sound sleeper. They are active at night and can make a quite a bit of noise including tapping of the shells. Also avoid areas that may be subject to extremes of temperature. Most other areas will be suitable for hermit crabs, although a nearby area where cleaning can be performed is generally a good idea. Spilling substrate on carpeting or carrying a heavy tank to another area of the house may prove undesirable. Some people will also complain of the smell of commercial diets or moist foods. Food odors shouldn't be significant if you feed your hermit crab small amounts but again this may be a factor when considering placement of the enclosure. Finally, never place your tank in sunlight. It will become excessively hot and your crabs will overheat and die.

ESCAPE

Land hermit crabs are notorious escape artists. If there is any possible way to get out of an enclosure, they will usually find it. In an aquarium, any structure that can allow them to reach the top edge will be investigated, so you need to carefully consider the placement of landscape structures. If you are using an open-top aquarium, make sure that wood and rock are in the center and not near the aquarium edges. As a general rule, it is a good idea to buy a screen cover for your hermit crab tank. It will help prevent any risk of escape and provide an area for you to place a light and for partially covering the top.

SUBSTRATE
In the wild, land hermit crabs are found in areas ranging from close to the shoreline, which is usually sandy and littered with shells and broken coral, to inland where there is a layer of humus/soil/leaf litter on the ground. In captivity, hermit crabs will fare well on sand, sand/soil mixes or aquarium gravel.

SAND
Most people select a fine grade (not powdery fine) sand because it is readily available in the pet trade and at large hardware stores. Play-sand works well. Use at least three inches (7 cm) of sand for smaller crabs and up to six inches (15 cm) for large ones. Make a depression in a corner and pour water slowly so that the bottom half of the sand layer is wet. There are two ways to provide water to your crabs in this kind of setup. Either you provide a shallow dish of freshwater or you can slope the sand so that a quarter of the tank has a depression you can pour water into. Simply add water to 50% of the height of the sand layer. As the water evaporates from the sand, it raises relative humidity. Hermit crabs will also be able to bury into the moist sand if they want to. In terms of ease of cleaning, a water dish is the better method of providing water. Sand is the preferred medium of most land hermit crab owners. Because it can become foul and smelly over time, regular replacement as needed is recommended.

GRAVEL
Gravel can be a functional and attractive substrate. You can pour a little water in the gravel layer to raise humidity. The problem with gravel is that it is not a good burrowing medium for hermit crabs who want to molt. So you need to include a plastic container (such as the type used for food storage) with a burrowing medium in your gravel bed setup (see Burrowing/Molting). When your tank gets too messy, gravel is easily washed clean. The plastic container with sand for burrowing can be easily removed to replace foul substrate. Gravel can be used successfully as a substrate for hermit crabs, but sand and sandy soil substrates are closer to what hermit crabs use in the wild.

HOW WET?
Hermit crabs are not rainforest creatures. They won't do well in soggy, wet enclosures. In the wild, the West Atlantic hermit crab is usually found in dry areas. The babies are often not too far from shore among shells, pieces of coral and detritus which dry quickly in the sun. Larger hermits are usually found more inland where there are trees, plants, driftwood and sandy soil. The sun, breezes and wind are all elements of the natural habitat that have drying effects. A good general rule is to keep the surface of your crab tank dry.

BURROWING/MOLTING SUBSTRATE
No matter how you keep your hermit crabs, you need to maintain an area

This is another setup showing the same features as the previous tank but here the freshwater section is created by sloping the sand and adding water. In this vivarium, a pair of Thailand freshwater crabs and a fiddler crab have also fared well. The final step is putting a screen cover and an incandescent bulb in a reflector type fixture to provide heat.

with a substrate that allows burrowing. The easiest way to do this is to place a wide and shallow flower pot or food storage container filled with either soil or a sand/soil mix. It should be slightly damp. Access to the container should be provided through a section of wood, cork bark and/or rock. By providing this burrowing container you will allow hermit crabs to burrow when they want and offer suitable conditions for molting.

LANDSCAPE AND DECORATION
CLIMBING AREAS

Hermit crabs can be very active at night and one of the things they like to do is climb. For this reason you should provide natural wood sections that are textured to permit easy climbing. Several kinds of wood are sold in the pet trade including driftwood, grapevine, fig wood and cholla cactus "skeleton". With the exception of driftwood, all of these woods should be kept on the dry land section or they will tend to mold and rot.

SHELTERS

In the wild, hermit crabs will often spend time in shelters, under logs, fallen leaves and other detritus as well as inside tree hollows and depressions in rock and burrows. Because relative humidity is higher in shelters and because shelters also provide protection from wind, they can help reduce evaporative water loss. A shelter also offers some protection from potential predators. Some land hermit crabs choose to molt in shelters instead of burrows. Cork bark is a light and attractive medium for creating a shelter but other material can be used, including oversized sea shells, coconut shell halves with a wedge knocked out as an entrance, and PVC pipe sections partially buried in substrate.

PLANTS

If introduced in pots that are accessible to the crabs, plants will eventually be uprooted and dry out as a result of the crabs' burrowing activities. Plants can also be eaten by hermit crabs. To decorate your hermit crab tank with plants, place them in either pots that cannot be accessed or glass jars of water with a foam cover. Good species for growing in water include arrowhead plants (*Syngonium*), pothos and Chinese evergreen (*Aglaonema*). These are readily available in plant stores and houseplant sections of department stores.

TEMPERATURE, HEATING AND LIGHTING

Land hermit crabs are found in subtropical and tropical areas. Because they are ectotherms, they depend on the temperature of their environment to maintain a body temperature that allows them to be active. Besides lack of water, the most common cause of death in land hermit crabs is too cool temperatures. Thousands die during the late fall, winter and early spring when homes are maintained too cool for too long to meet the needs of hermit crabs. If you have been to south Florida during the winter you have an idea of what the lower range of temperature tolerance is for land hermit crabs. In the wild, hermit crabs can seek shelter from bad weather by taking advantage of a variety of microhabitats, such as the inside of tree hollows and burrows, and under decomposing vegetation, with temperatures that may be more favorable than air temperature.

A temperature of 76-82°F (24-28°C) is ideal for high activity and feeding in hermit crabs. To maintain that range, most people will have to provide a heat source. Because a heating unit will take up a certain amount of space, it soon becomes clear why the small plastic terraria often sold as hermit crab homes are not suitable for keeping these creatures. The most widely used heating sources for hermit crabs are incandescent light bulbs. They can be placed in a reflector type fixture over a screen covered all-glass enclosure. The night lights and red incandescent bulbs sold for reptiles are good alternatives to regular incandescent bulbs during cool months because they can be kept on all night. For smaller tanks of five to ten gallons, incandescent aquarium strip reflectors will also work well. But in the larger size tanks, standard elongated incandescent aquarium bulbs may not generate enough heat. If you have a tank of 29 gallons or larger, an economic alternative is to use a ceramic infrared heating bulb sold in the reptile section of pet stores. When using incandescent or infrared lighting over hermit crabs, selecting the right wattage bulb will be critical to prevent overheating.

Another way to heat a hermit crab tank is to use a subtank heating pad or heat mat. These heating units, sold in the reptile sections of pet stores, fit under a glass tank. If you plan on using this, remember that the heating pad should cover no more than a third of the floor area so that crabs can get away from excess heat when they want. The other consideration is that you should use only a shallow layer of gravel when using this kind of heater. If you use a deep substrate, the heater will be relatively ineffective and there will be a risk of the heater cracking the bottom of the aquarium.

Sand, because of its density, can form an insulation layer that will prevent heat from rising to the surface and will cause it to build up at the glass level. This will make the bottom glass pane of the aquarium expand to the degree that it may crack.

At low temperatures, 74°F (23°C) and below, hermit crabs will become less active and feed little, if at all. They can survive cool temperatures in the 60's for brief periods of time, but if kept long-term at suboptimal temperatures, they will eventually die. Remember, a temperature of 76-84°F (24-29°C) is ideal for land hermit crabs.

THERMOMETER
There is only one way to know what the temperature is in your hermit crab tank, and that is to use a thermometer. Several kinds are now sold in the pet trade, ranging from inexpensive stick-on types to dial and glass thermometers. You can also buy digital thermometers in some department stores or electronic supply stores. Place the thermometer at ground level under the heat source, in the case of a light bulb, or over the heat source if a heating pad is used.

LIGHTING
Because most hermit crabs spend the day concealed in some kind of shelter, no additional lighting should be required to keep your hermit crabs

If you must use a plastic terrarium for keeping hermit crabs you should still provide three inches of sand when housing small hermit crabs. The sand should be moistened. Two water dishes and a shelter complete the setup.

Side shot of vivarium showing plants in a glass jar of water and active hermit crabs.

It is important to offer hermit crabs shelters where the may hide during the day.

Hermit crabs gathered on a wood section in the early evening.

healthy. However, there are anecdotal reports that hermit crabs may bene-
fit from brief weekly exposure to the sun or to high UV-B fluorescent reptile bulbs. The value of a UV-A or UV-B light source as a tool for successfully keeping hermit crabs needs to be further investigated. If you decide
to expose your crabs to sunlight, place them in an aluminum screen cage
or in a fine wire-mesh cage. Do not place glass-sided or plastic hermit crab
enclosures in the sun. The cages will overheat and the hermit crabs will
die.

**South American *C. compressus* must be offered brackish water in addition to fresh
water to fare well in captivity.**

SHELLS

From the time they are land-dwelling, hermit crabs depend on a shell to provide protection and to store water. Finding the right shell is critical to the survival of a land hermit crab and only a hermit crab can determine if a shell has the right fit. Shells preferred by hermit crabs form concentric spiral coils. They are broad on the outside and become narrower as they coil toward the center. The opening of the shell is more or less round. A good shell will allow a hermit crab to withdraw into it and effectively seal access to vulnerable body parts with the crab's large claw and second walking leg. Water holding capacity, snugness, weight and drag when moving are probably all factors in the selection of what a hermit crab eventually considers a good home.

Generally, the opening of the shell should be slightly larger than the large claw but other factors such as shell structure will be considered by the hermit crab. Besides providing a shelter, the home shell is also an important water storage structure. Finding a shell that can be well-sealed by the abdomen to hold stored water is critical to the welfare of a hermit crab. Generally, spiral coiling, broadly conical sea-shells are the best choices for hermit crabs. You should have several extra shells including some that are about the same size and others that are somewhat larger than what your hermit crab currently lives in. As your hermit crab grows, it will require increasingly larger shells to call home.

Because we are not qualified to determine what is the best fitting shell for a hermit crab, the only thing we can do is to offer a variety of shells and let it pick out the one it prefers. In the pet trade, turbo shells and murex are the most commonly sold shells for hermit crabs. The shells of land snails and tree snails will also work for smaller specimens. Shells can be bought either from businesses that specialize in hermit crabs or from shell shops.

A good shell is critically important to hermit crabs and they will spend time investigating other shells, trying them out and so on. Empty shells, for good reasons, are fascinating to hermit crabs.

CLEANING SHELLS
It is a good idea to disinfect new shells or shells previously used by hermit crabs by boiling them in water for about 15 minutes. Let them cool and empty the water from shells before introducing them into the tank.

FANCY SHELLS
The external appearance of a shell is of minor importance to a hermit crab but is often important to owners. If pretty shells will enhance the time you spend observing and enjoying your hermit crab, then by all means buy and place nice shells in your tank. There are now many select, ornamental shells sold for hermit crabs in the pet trade.

An assortment of shells should be included in a hermit crab setup. Providing attractive shells will add to the aesthetic appearance of hermit crabs.

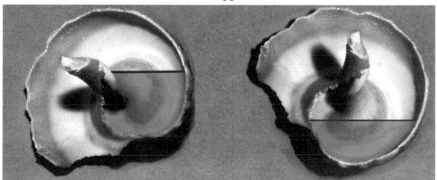

This is a cut out sea-shell showing where water would be stored. The water level rises when a hermit crab backs into its shell and allows moistening of the gills (left). When the hermit crab emerges from its shell, the water settles to a lower level (right). This also allows space for a hermit crab to fill its shell with more water

SHELL-LESS

In the wild, hermit crabs out of their shells are vulnerable to dehydration and predators. They will not survive long when shell-less. The same is true in captivity, which is why it's critical that you make available a variety of shells for your crab. Whenever a hermit crab finds a new shell, the animal must condition it to fit its needs. This means grooming parts of the shell and accumulating a water reservoir with the proper ion concentration. Hermit crabs sometimes leave an old shell, try a new shell and then decide the new shell is not so great after all and go back to the former shell. The search for the perfect shell is one of the hermit crab's endeavors in life. Because in nature large shells are less common than small shells, one of the problems that larger hermit crabs encounter is the inability to find shells large enough to accommodate them. That is one reason why very large hermit crabs are relatively uncommon.

WATER

Hermit crabs, like most animals, require water to survive. Failure to provide water is probably the most common cause of death in captive animals. Although the hermit crab is no longer adapted to living in water, it does need to carry water wherever it goes. Water is stored in the borrowed gastropod (snail) shell it calls home. The tight sealing abdominal portion of the crab plays a key role in sealing in shell water. Shell water is maintained by dipping into a body of water or by drinking. To drink, land hermit crabs do not usually dip their mouths in water but instead transfer water to the mouth using their small claw. Water that is ingested through drinking can be drawn into the branchial (gill) chambers and expelled into the shell.

Hermit crabs, however, do not depend exclusively on the availability of water from a dish. They also obtain water from food such as vegetation, fruit and the flesh of other animals. Because they also tend to store fat, they can probably obtain metabolic water from the breakdown of fat. There is also speculation that water may be obtained from moist substrate.

Generally, West Atlantic hermit crabs fare best on fresh water or brackish water (up to 50% sea water) but will not usually fare well long-term if given exclusively full strength sea water. In captivity, they should be given both dechlorinated (buy dechlorinator/dechloraminator tablets at a pet store), high-quality fresh water and brackish water (five tablespoons of rock salt or seawater mix per gallon of water) in separate shallow dishes, such as the reptile food and water dishes now sold in the pet trade. Do not use deep dishes with smooth sides. In deep containers, the crabs will have difficulty accessing the water and may drown if they fall into the dish. A good water level is about half the height of the crab in the shell when at rest. In deeper dishes or containers, place rocks in the water to allow the crabs to climb out easily. The water should be changed every one to two days or whenever fouled. It is important that you monitor the water level to make sure that water is available at all times. Too often I see pet stores display hermit crabs on a dry substrate with no water. That is a primary reason why many pet stores lose large numbers of hermit crabs.

WHY BRACKISH WATER?
Many books for good reasons recommend that only freshwater be offered to hermit crabs. They will in fact do fine with freshwater, as long as they have a source of salts in their diet or environment. Remember that the water in the shell is maintained at a certain ion concentration that is adjusted through behaviors, drinking of water and ingestion of salts. Given a choice of both fresh and brackish waters, a hermit crab will select what it feels it needs for proper hydration. The normal course is for hermit crabs to select freshwater but after acquiring a new shell, a hermit crab may initially select brackish water to maintain the proper ion concentration in the stored water of the new shell. Because we cannot control ion and water bal-

ance in hermit crabs, the best course is to provide conditions that allow them to select what they prefer. So I recommend two types of water, fresh and brackish, in separate dishes.

WATER PH AND HARDNESS

I add crushed coral to the water area to increase water hardness and raise pH. In a sloped tank I edge the water section with crushed coral sold for marine aquaria. I also recommend placing a small amount of crushed coral in water dishes. Other hermit crab owners have recommended that cuttlefish bone or a seashell be placed in water.

MISTING

In nature, hermit crabs tend to be particularly active following rains. For this reason it is recommended that they be lightly misted on a daily basis in the early evening. To prevent the accumulation of mineral stains on the walls of the enclosure, use purified water (available bottled at supermarkets and drugs stores) when misting. Misting will provide water for drinking and help raise the relative humidity.

DAILY DIPPING

Many books recommend daily dipping of hermit crabs into water. This is done to ensure that a hermit crab gets enough water and keeps its gills wet. This may be especially valuable for newly purchased hermit crabs because many are dehydrated. But it should not be necessary if you keep your crabs in a well-designed setup. The secret to a land hermit crab being able to survive away from water is that it carries water within its shell. For its gills to function properly, the necessary water is obtained from that stored within the shell. When a hermit crab backs into its shell, the volume of the abdomen displaces stored water, causing it to rise and bathe the gills. A healthy crab doesn't need daily dipping. However a hermit crab does more than just carry water; it also regulates the concentration of salts in shell water. By dipping a crab in freshwater you are assuming that you know better than the crab how much freshwater it needs and that you also know better the best course of action to maintain ion concentrations in the shell water. If kept in the right kind of setup, daily dipping of crabs is unnecessary.

RELATIVE HUMIDITY

Relative humidity is a measure of how much water is contained in air as water vapor. Relative humidity is measured by a device called a hygrometer. Generally, hermit crabs do best at 78-90% relative humidity. One of the effects of high relative humidity is that it reduces the rate at which evaporative water is lost. As temperatures drop in the evening, some of the water in the air may condense and provide a source of water. In short, a hermit crab will be able to conserve water and will be less likely to dehydrate in a high humidity environment. Any one who has been to south Florida or the Caribbean knows the high humidity of the hermit crab's native habitat.

The first step to raising relative humidity is to create an evaporative water source. If you use a deep substrate, keeping the bottom layer moist will provide an area from which water will be able to evaporate. If you have a shallow dry substrate you can introduce a sponge humidifier to increase air humidity. This is simply a piece of polyurethane foam or sponge you can place in a shallow container of water. The high surface area of the foam will allow water to evaporate at a good rate. A very effective way to raise the relative humidity is to mist the tank nightly, using purified water to prevent the accumulation of mineral stains on the glass. As the water evaporates, the air humidity rises. To stabilize humidity in your hermit crab tank, you should also cover the half of the tank's top which is not occupied by a heat light. A piece of plexiglass cut to size works well as a tank cover. As a quick and temporary measure you can use a piece of clear plastic wrap, being careful not to place it beneath the light source.

VENTILATION

Notice that I only recommend covering part of the top of the enclosure. Hermit crabs will usually not do well in sealed wet environments such as a closed terrarium. Wind or breeze and a dry substrate surface are features of their natural habitats. A sealed environment will also speed the growth of molds and bacteria in the tank. Allow for air flow.

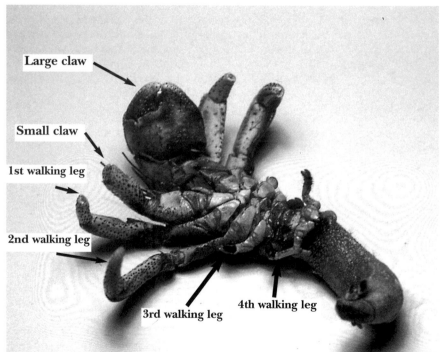

This photo shows the ventral (belly) side of a hermit crab. Notice the cheliped (claws), the large front two pairs of walking legs and behind these, the reduced third and fourth walking legs. The leg-like third maxillipeds are visible between the claws in the mouth area. A hermit crab anchors into its shell using the reduced third and fourth walking legs and the uropods at the end of the abdomen.

FEEDING YOUR HERMIT CRAB

Hermit crabs are opportunistic scavenging omnivores which can eat a wide range of foods, from fruit and vegetation to insects, carrion and even feces. They have a good sense of smell and are capable of locating food several feet by using olfactory cues. Foods with potent smells, such as ripe fruit or a dead animal, are recognized readily.

In captivity, food should be offered in shallow dishes to prevent rapid fouling of the tank. Hermit crabs aren't the neatest eaters in the world so you will need to perform an occasional tank clean-up. Hermit crabs, if one studies their anatomy, have a small gut. This means that they will eat very small amounts per feeding session. For this reason you only need to offer small portions of food when feeding these crabs. Excess food will simply go to waste and end up rotting and smelling up whatever room the crabs are kept in.

There are now several commercial hermit crab diets that will form a good base diet for your animals. However, all hermit crab foods are not created equally. Some commercial diets will not be liked by your crab. Other diets, even if eaten by your crabs, may stink and be intolerable to you while others yet will be relished and acceptable to both crab and man. If your hermit crab does not like one brand of hermit crab

Food dish with a variety of foods including grape, dried date, commercial hermit crab diet, spirulina flakes. The grape has a light coating of calcium carbonate.

food, then try another. Tropical fish flakes and fish foods are good alternatives to hermit crab diets as are moistened dog foods and pieces of fish or shrimp with the shell on. Hermit crabs will also eat dead insects including the freeze-dried flies and crickets now sold in the reptile sections of pet stores. Pre-killed mealworms and crickets sold in the pet trade coated with calcium can be offered for variety. Hermit crabs also feed on plant matter, including romaine, which has a good level of calcium, and fruit such as grapes (one of their favorites), apple, bananas and papaya. Hermit crabs also enjoy dried fruit and have a particular preference for dates and raisins.

TREATS
Hermit crabs like fatty foods as well as foods with a nutty odor. These should be offered in moderation as part of a varied diet. Two of their

favorites are raw coconut and peanut butter. When I was looking for various land hermit crabs on the small islands of New Caledonia, I would put sections of open coconut on stakes along various trails during the day. At night, swarms of hermit crabs, including the occasional coconut crab, gathered to feed on the coconut. I also experimented with gobs of peanut butter and had even greater success.

A big favorite of hermit crabs is pop corn. Place a few popped kernels in your tank at night and watch your hermits come to life. Other treats that may be beneficial for hermit crabs include salty foods such as crackers, particularly cheese-flavored varieties.

SUPPLEMENTS
Little is known of the nutritional requirements of hermit crabs but by feeding them a varied diet, most of their required nutrients will be provided. The one supplement that I recommend is calcium in the form of powdered calcium carbonate such as crushed oyster shell, and cuttlefish bone.

MAINTENANCE SCHEDULES
Keeping hermit crabs healthy requires regular maintenance schedules.

DAILY TASKS:
• Check you hermit crabs without removing animals from shelters or burrows.
• Provide small amounts of food and clean water. The food and water containers should be washed when dirty using an antibacterial dish detergent and THOROUGHLY rinsed before use.
• Scattered food debris should be removed as well as fecal material observed on the substrate surface.
• Mist your hermit crabs at least once in the early evening.

MONTHLY TASKS (OR AS NEEDED):
• Replace substrate.
• Replace damaged or dead plants.
• Replace or clean landscape materials as needed. If a 5% bleach solution is used as a disinfectant to clean landscape materials, allow them to sit overnight in a container of clean water after rinsing to remove all traces of bleach and detergent.
• Clean sides of tank.

Did you know?
Hermit crabs excrete urine through antennal glands, located at the base of the antennae.

MOLTING

As for other crustaceans such as shrimp and lobster, hermit crabs molt (shed their integument) on a regular basis as they grow. During a molt cycle, four stages occur. During the first stage (*proecdysis* or *premolt*), the new integument is formed beneath the old one, water is absorbed in the body, and calcium as well as other nutrients is absorbed from the exoskeleton. The second stage (*ecdysis/molt*) is the actual molting process. The old integument/exoskeleton is shed off and the crab increases its size by absorbing water. Right after a molt a hermit crab will appear pink and will be very soft and vulnerable. The third stage (*postmolt*) allows the new integument to harden into an exoskeleton. Stored calcium and nutrients are mobilized, the old shell is eaten and food and water are ingested to supply lost calcium and the nutrients necessary for the new larger body. The new exoskeleton hardens. The end result is a slightly larger crab that will eventually have to hunt for a new larger shell. The fourth stage of the molting cycle is the period between molts and is called the *intermolt* period. In the wild, adult hermit crabs molt once a year. In captivity, several factors affect the molt cycle, including steady availability of food.

The hermit crab remains in the shell during most of the molt. Both in the wild and in captivity, hermit crabs select secure places to molt such as natural shelters — under fallen wood or litter, or in burrows excavated in the substrate. They may remain in burrows for up to two weeks before molting. A hermit crab will remain in its shell during most of the molt. Following molting, a hermit crab increases its body volume by absorbing water. Because a great deal of body calcium is lost during the molting process, a hermit crab will consume its molted exoskeleton to quickly regain some of the lost calcium. Thus, you should not remove the skin of a crab that has just molted.

PREVENTING MOLT-RELATED DEATHS

In general, molting is a vulnerable period for hermit crabs. A small percentage of hermit crabs both in the wild and in captivity die during the molting process. One of the great difficulties in keeping the coconut crab, which is the largest of the hermit crabs, is providing the conditions that allow molting. For this giant species, a substrate depth of about two feet will be required. In captivity, the risk of hermit crabs dying during molting is high because of five factors:

    1) Not enough water has been provided. As mentioned before, dehydration is probably the most common cause of death of hermit crabs in captivity.

    2) Excessive handling. Owners are concerned when they see their crab hidden and inactive for days on end and they feel compelled to dig it out of its molting refuge and handle it. Handling a hermit crab during molting can cause fatal harm.

3) The exoskeleton, an important source of calcium, is removed following molting.

4) No shelter or refuge is provided. Hermit crabs like to dig in soft substrate such as a soil/sand mix when molting or to seek access in a shelter.

5) Cannibalism. A hermit crab that is kept with other crabs which aren't fed adequately or are much larger, housed with inadequate shelter, or is injured in the molting process may be cannibalized.

MOLTING SCHEDULES

Small, immature hermit crabs will molt several times a year but as they grow older and larger, they may molt only every 12-18 months depending on various conditions such as temperature, diet and injury. Prior to molting, a land hermit crab will hide in a burrow or shelter for about two weeks. Once the old exoskeleton has been cast, a hermit crab has a pale body color and will be very soft and vulnerable to both predators and contact injuries (do not handle). So if by chance out of impatience you find your hermit crab pale and soft with the old exoskeleton next to it, do not disturb it but do cover it with a shelter. Over the next seven to ten days following molting, a hermit crab will eat its molted exoskeleton and regain some of the calcium required for its new exoskeleton to harden. When all is said and done you're looking at three to four weeks for a molt cycle to be completed.

REGENERATION OF LOST LIMBS

The life of a crab is hazardous and loss of, or damage to, limbs, claws or antennae may occur. Like other crabs, hermit crabs have the ability to regenerate a leg or limb sections severed at a joint over several molts.

OTHER BEHAVIORS

SOUND PRODUCTION

Anyone who has kept hermit crabs will tell you they're noisy little critters. If kept in a bedroom they can keep you awake with their clanging around as they climb or bang against glass and shuffle among shells.

A section of driftwood was lifted to expose this buried hermit crab.

Land hermit crabs also produce clicking sounds by intentionally tapping the shells and rapping legs as well as make stridulating sounds by rubbing legs together. This noise-making is used in hermit crab communication, including aggressive displays. If a hermit crab tries to climb onto another or makes contact with it, both crabs may stridulate in annoyance.

DEFENSE

The normal defensive response of a hermit crab is to withdraw into its shell and seal the opening with the enlarged left claw and third walking leg. They will perform this withdrawal response in reaction to perceived movement by large moving objects (potential predators). In the wild, you can see this behavior close to shore where babies, as they suddenly back into their shells, may roll a little ways if they are on a slope. Hermit crabs in trees will also withdraw in their shells when they feel threatened, often causing them to fall to the ground. If picked up, some hermit crabs withdraw in their shells while others may emerge from their shells ready to move or, if necessary, pinch what they can grab.

AUTOTOMY

If threatened, hermit crabs can cast off a limb. Hypothetically, this can hold the attention of a predator as the crab scuttles away. In captivity, autotomy is often witnessed with dying crabs. The latter will drop a claw or leg more readily than a healthy one and will sometimes do so for no apparent cause.

ANTENNA ACTIVITY

Hermit crabs are not the most expressive animals in the world but their level of activity can give you an indication of what motivates and excites them. In general, when in the presence of food or when following olfactory cues, they will display a high level of antenna activity, dipping them down and up.

GROOMING

Land hermit crabs perform various grooming behaviors including keeping the eyestalks and the antennas free of dirt and debris. Specialized brush-like structures (setae) on mouth-parts (third maxillipeds) are used to groom the antennae and eye stalks. The various legs also groom each other to various degrees. The back legs are used to groom the shell and its edges.

DEFECATION

A question sometimes asked by puzzled keepers concerns hermit crab defecation. Do they defecate in the shell? The answer is, **no**, they do not defecate in their shells but curve their abdomens so as to defecate out of the shell. Fecal matter can sometimes be seen on the substrate surface in the form of thin fecal strings.

HANDLING

The best way to pick up a hermit crab is to hold it by the back of the shell, keeping fingers away from the claws. There is really no need to handle a hermit crab any other way. However, some owners decide they want to allow their hermit crabs to crawl on their hands. If you are one of those, my advice is to start with small hermit crabs, making sure you hold your hand flat. Do this over a table or a cushioned area. The problem with handling hermit crabs in this manner is that they can readily fall from a flat palm and injure themselves. Falls from several feet onto a hard floor usually result in fatal injuries.

Another risk of free-handling a hermit crab is being seized by a claw and pinched. Some hermit crabs are ready pinchers. Others, if they feel as if they are falling or threatened, may hold onto skin with their claws. Hermit crabs have a very painful pinch. I have seen more than one child trying to maintain their composure as their pet hermit crabs are locked onto the skin between the thumb and index finger. With small crabs this hurts, but a larger hermit crab has more crushing power and will make you sweat with pain as you grit your teeth and try to remain cool. To get a hermit crab to release its grip, put it under lukewarm running water or dunk your hand into a container, such as a bucket or a sink filled with lukewarm water and wait. Eventually it will let go.

Hermit crabs vary in their readiness to use their claws to pinch. Some owners claim that with handling a hermit crab becomes less likely to pinch. If you really need an animal that can be handled with regularity, there are much better choices than hermit crabs.

BREEDING

Because of the difficulty rearing newly hatched hermit crabs, these neat animals are usually not bred in captivity. It is simply easier to manage wild population of hermit crabs. Nonetheless the breeding pattern of hermit crabs is worth knowing about because it will give you insights into the reproduction of crustaceans.

Mating usually occurs near the shoreline and large numbers of land hermit crabs migrate toward the shore for breeding. During mating, both crabs extend partially out of the shell and copulation occurs ventral to ventral (belly to belly) with the male passing a spermatophore to the female. Following mating and later fertilization, the eggs, which may number up to 50,000, are released by females along the shoreline. After the eggs hatch, newborn hermit crabs start off as tiny sea-dwelling plankton called zoeae (aquatic larvae). The aquatic larval/planktonic stage lasts about a month. Then there is a stage where the tiny hermit crabs are aquatic but already seek tiny shells as their home. They then reach land and eventually transfer to shells on the shore. Once established on land, it requires about two years for baby land hermit crabs to become sexually mature adults.

DISEASE

Like most organisms, hermit crabs are subject to a variety of diseases ranging from nutritional disorders to parasites to various infections. However,
little work has been done on identifying the early stages of disease and the
most effective treatments. Generally, the best procedure is to prevent disease by providing good care to your hermit crab.

SIGNS OF ILLNESS

There are two common signs of illness in a hermit crab — sluggishness and
little or no movement of antennae. A dying hermit crab doesn't have the
energy to behave normally. It barely has the strength to anchor into its
shell and may even have dragged itself out of the shell. In virtually all cases,
if your basic husbandry is correct, then there will be little you can do to
save the poor hermit crab. Even in cases where poor husbandry, such as
dehydration, may be a factor, damage to the crab from lack of water will
often be beyond repair.

DISEASES RELATED TO HUSBANDRY

Providing a hermit crab with its basic requirements will be essential to prevent disease:

• Temperature. Hermit crabs are subtropical to tropical creatures.
It is common for hermit crabs to die during the cold winter months when
not enough heat is provided. Conversely, hermit crabs will die if a tank is
overheated.

• Hydration. I so often see hermit crabs in pet shops displayed
with no water that it is safe to say that many members of the public also
neglect water when caring for their hermit crabs. Dehydrating hermit
crabs will initially choose to tightly withdraw within the shell to reduce
water loss, but later, even if dipped in water, may be too damaged to recover. A sign that a crab is dehydrated is that it will emerge and spend long
periods in water when placed in it but will be relatively sluggish with little
or no fluttering of antennae. The likelihood for these crabs to recover is
poor. This is one of the most common causes of death in hermit crabs. Use
a routine for maintenance of your animals, misting them nightly and providing them with an easily accessible water dish.

• Relative humidity. This is a vital part of providing hermit crabs
with enough water. Humidity should be 79-90%, but the subtrate surface
of your crab tanks should be relatively dry, and certainly not soggy.

• Burrowing. Failure to provide a burrowing medium for molting
is a common cause of death. Land hermit crabs need a place to burrow.

• Diet. Hermit crabs have nutritional requirements, including a
need for dietary calcium. Feed them a varied and high quality diet. Making
available salt in the form of brackish water can also be beneficial.

• Cleanliness. Keeping the enclosure clean, including regularly
providing fresh water and food in clean containers, will be important for
the long-term health of your hermit crab.

Certain aerosol sprays such as hair spray and household cleaners can have
a harmful effect on hermit crabs. Do not keep crabs in areas where such
sprays are used.

OTHER DISEASES

In the wild, hermit crabs are parasitized by flies and mites. In captivity, mites are sometimes found on hermit crabs. Because many miticides are potentially toxic to hermit crabs, getting rid of mites is difficult. Crabs can be dipped in sea water. Mites can be removed individually by applying a section of rolled Scotch tape to the mite. Generally any infestation of mites will require procedures to prevent their spread and reinfection. This means keeping crabs in simply designed enclosures that are regularly cleaned, with all materials replaced on a regular basis.

Little is known of the other diseases of hermit crabs and even less about how to treat them. Some owners, when hermit crabs appear sluggish and ill, use a "shotgun approach", dipping them once or twice daily in antibiotic solutions used for treating fish. The effectiveness of these treatments has yet to be determined.

The right way to hold a land hermit crab.

OTHER LAND HERMIT CRABS

Birgus latro: **The king of the hermit crabs**

Very rarely, live young specimens of the coconut crab, also known as the robber crab, are imported into the U.S. and offered by reptile dealers. There are two forms — the red coconut crab and the black coconut crab. Red specimens, such as some of the ones from Aldabra, are a brilliant orange-red. Coconut crabs are impressive and can make quite a display in public zoos and aquaria. Unlike typical land hermit crabs, the coconut crab stops using a shell after the first year of life. This allows it to grow without being dependent on the availability of large shells. Very large coconut crabs may be over forty years old and weigh more than eight pounds. As the name indicates, coconut is a favorite food. They are also known as robber crabs because of their habits of stealing objects and food to later test their edibility. I was once awakened in my tent by a coconut crab testing my big toe as it rested against a mosquito net. As could be expected, I awakened startled. Although impressive, this species is not well suited for most people unless one can provide large enclosures. The general requirements of hermit crabs have to be met, but on a much larger scale. You need heat between 76 and 84°F (24-29°C) and relative humidity of 70–85%. You also need a fair amount of ground area with large-scale shelters and large water containers. On the rare occasions when I found coconut crabs during the day, they were inside tree hollows or in deep burrows. On a couple of occasions in dark forests, I have also found coconut crabs clinging to the sides of a tree during the day. At night, coconut crabs like climbing areas such as tree sections. In fact, they are remarkable climbers. I had one that tore open the bag I had it in and climbed straight up the edge of a partition to the ceiling of a hotel room. These crabs are active, very strong, and extremely talented escape artists. They will easily tear up wire mesh. They also need a deep substrate where they can burrow during molting, allowing them to make their three-foot long and one- or two-feet deep molting burrows. Adults molt about once a year during the winter. They remain buried for more than month during molting. In general, coconut crabs have been short-lived in captivity and protocols for consistent long-term maintenance still have to be developed. Surprisingly few public aquaria and zoos have them on display. All and all, this is a very impressive species that deserves more research on captive rearing of young animals.

OTHER LAND HERMIT CRABS

There are several other species of land hermit crabs, some of which are more colorful and attractive than the West Atlantic hermit crabs commonly sold. Considering the vagaries of the pet trade, it may well be that some of these exotic land hermit crabs could become available in the future. The general maintenance of most land hermit crabs will follow the basic pattern presented in this book.

Coconut crab (Birgus latro), the largest of the terrestrial arthropods, photographed in the author's room in New Caledonia. After one year of age, the coconut crab no longer carries a home shell. Large specimens can weigh up to seven pounds.

There is some variation in *C. compressus*. This is an example of a light phased specimen. Because this species frequently ventures inland, it can be found in the shells of land snails.

OTHER CRABS SOLD IN THE FRESHWATER AQUARIUM TRADE

RED-CLAWED FRESHWATER CRABS

These small Asian crabs are usually displayed in aquaria with no access to land. They typically are dead within a few weeks. I have housed them in a sloped sand setup with a section of water, in a tank with small hermit crabs. Interestingly, these crabs spend a great deal of time on land, thus they should be kept in a shoreline type vivarium. They enjoy dead crickets and fish flakes. They are best kept in a setup dedicated to them because they are vulnerable to predation following a molt. Nonetheless, in a large enough setup which is not too crowded, they can be kept with small hermit crabs and their high level of activity can enliven a hermit crab setup.

FIDDLER CRABS (*UCA* SPECIES)

Fiddler crabs are usually displayed in pet stores in aquatic freshwater tanks with no access to land. Several species are now offered, and the basic characteristics for care are the same. Males have an enlarged claw, usually white, while females have two diminutive claws. Fiddler crabs will only survive a few weeks under the conditions used by most stores for display. They should be maintained in setups where crabs have access to a land area of rock or wood. They need some salt in the water. There are reports of individuals kept alive for a year or more in water with only one to two tablespoons of rock salt or seawater mix per gallon. In the wild, fiddler crabs

Some hermit crabs are imported from South America including Ecuador. The species found on the west coast of South America is *Coenobita compressus*. This is a hardy and attractive species which, if kept warm and humid enough, will be active during the day. The only drawback is that it only grows to 40 grams.

live in areas with sea water or brackish water e.g. 50% seawater. They molt in water. The biggest problem with fiddler crabs is provision of an adequate diet. Fiddler crabs are deposit feeders and incapable of breaking up chunks of food for ingestion. The best technique is to have a substrate of sand or fine aquarium gravel and offer powdered flake food. The crabs will process fine sand through their mouths and sift out biological material.

This land crab (probably *Gecarcinus*)is imported from Central America and sold in the pet trade as a " moon crab". It requires heat, humidity and at least twelve inches of sand with the bottom third water saturated. They generally can be kept like hermit crabs, except that all caging materials from enclosures to water dishes need to be on a larger scale.

Red phase of the "moon crab".

Fiddler crabs have been successfully kept with small fish in brackish water setups that have a "land area" of either rock or wood emerging from the water.

LAND CRABS

Recently, land crabs, usually members of the genus *Cardisoma* or *Gecarcinus,* have been offered in the pet trade and sometimes sold in kits consisting of an extra large plastic terrarium with sand and a small water dish. They will not survive long under such conditions. These large crabs require at least a 36-inch long tank with six inches of sand as bottom substrate and another six to 12 inches of moistened soil/sand mix on top. The bottom sand layer should be kept wet because land crabs need to burrow into the water-line when molting. Land crabs need heat, shelters and high humidity. They are omnivorous, as are land hermit crabs. Land crabs need a shallow pan of water. They are only recommended for the dedicated individuals willing to provide the space and conditions required.